VEGETABLE PRESERVATION AND MORE

Effortless ball canning recipes. Make

home canning and preserving easy.
Save all the nutritions in a proper way.

HEATHER LOMBARD

Disclaimer

Please note the information contained within this document is for educational and entertainment purposes only. All effort has been executed to present accurate, up-to-date, and reliable, complete information. No warranties of any kind are declared or implied. Readers acknowledge that the author is not engaging in the rendering of legal, financial, medical, or professional advice. The content within this book has been derived from various sources. Please consult a licensed professional before attempting any techniques outlined in this book.

By reading this document, the reader agrees that under no circumstances is the author responsible for any losses, direct or indirect, which are incurred as a result of the use of the information contained within this document, including, but not limited to, — errors, omissions, or inaccuracies.

© **Copyright 2021 - All rights reserved.**

The content contained within this book may not be reproduced, duplicated, or transmitted without direct written permission from the author or the publisher.

Under no circumstances will any blame or legal responsibility be held against the publisher, or author, for any damages, reparation, or monetary loss due to the information contained within this book. Either directly or indirectly. You are responsible for your own choices, actions, and results.

TABLE OF CONTENTS

Disclaimer 2

Description 5

Introduction 7

Canning Food Basics 9

    What is Canning? 9

    What about Food Preservation 9

    History Of Canning 10

    Why Can Your Food? 12

    Getting Prepared For Canning and Preserving 14

Canning Equipment 17

    Canning Supplies You Need For Home Canning 17

Dos and Don'ts For Home Canning 23

    Dos 23

    Don'ts 24

    Steps For Water Bath Canning 25

    Mistakes You Can Prevent 27

    Reasons Why You Can't Afford To Not 29

Water Bath Canning Vs. Pressure Canning 32

    Importance of Using Labels 35

Food Preservation Techniques 38

    Preserving Fruits The Proper Way 41

    Strawberries 42

    Tomatoes 44

    Cabbage 45

    Hot peppers formula 47

    Lemons 50

    Green Beans 51

Benefits Derived From Canning And Preserving Food 54

    Deciding What's Right For You 56

    Sterilizing jars for canning 58

Precautions When Canning Starchy Foods 63

Emergency Food 68

    Simple, Safe, And Delicious 68

    Natural Food Preservatives 70

    Classification Of Natural Food Preservatives 70

    Some Traditional Practices Of Food Preservation 72

    10 Uses For Used Canning Lids 73

    1. Versatile 73

    2. Coordinating game 74

    3. Windchime 74

    4. Kids' toy 74

    5. Scarecrow 74

    6. Fridge magnets 75

    7. Blends in a container 75

    8. Dry Goods Storage 75

    9. Christmas Yard Art 75

    10. Christmas trimmings 75

    Why Canning is Making a Comeback 76

    Surviving the Upcoming Food Crisis 77

Conclusion/Final Remarks 81

Description

Learn How to Prepare Tastiest Food That Will Last You a Lifetime

With This Canning Cookbook.

There's nothing like opening the pantry or freezer door on a frigid winter's day, where the snow – already up to the window sills – is coming down so hard you can't see your mailbox, and finding row upon row of neatly labeled produce and meats and remembering once again that if the world ended outside your door, your family would still eat well.

Equip your pantry and freezer with the tastiest foods with the help of this cookbook.

This book is made for the beginner canners who want to enjoy the pleasures of pickling, preserving, and making unusual taste treats of all sorts in small batches during any time of the year. The recipes are made for beginners, and every step is explained in a detailed manner - you'll never wonder, "What to do next?"

Enjoy the foods that are hard to find during "off-season" all year long.

A good portion of the recipes can be refrigerated instead of being sealed in jars, which is a boon especially in the winter months when canning supplies are often difficult to find.

Bonus - all of these recipes will provide you with tasty and unusual treats that are perfect to give as gifts.

Here's what this canning cookbook will offer you:

- Beginner's guide to canning (with detailed methods)
- Tasty recipes for pickling (dills, onions, carrots, etc.)
- Mouthwatering recipes for fruit juices, jams, jellies, and marmalades
- Guide for long-time preservation
- And much more!

If you want to enjoy your favorite food all year long, even during "off-season," this guide will show you how. All you have to do is to follow simple step-by-step instructions – it's that easy.

Scroll up, click on "Buy Now with 1-Click", and Get Your Copy Now!

Introduction

Thank you for downloading *"Canning And Preserving: Preserving Foods At The Comfort Of Your Home."*

Have you seen other's pantry shelves brimming with home-canned goods, and you would like to do the same? Or you would like to find out how to make jam to give as Christmas gifts this year. Whatever your reason, canning is a skill that is very well worth the effort.

Not too long back in our recent past, before the arrival of refrigeration, the preservation of the harvest often meant the difference between survival and starvation. Our ancestors developed and used many ingenious methods to make sure that they had food year-round. Root cellars, brining and fermenting, canning and preserving, smoking, salting, and drying were all used for various fruits, vegetables, meats, fish, poultry, and eggs. With careful planning, much diligence, and a little co-operation from Mother Nature, a year-round food supply was assured.

One of the advantages of canning is how convenient it is. Once you have canned anything, whether it is a vegetable, a relish, or a jam, it is very easy to grab one off the shelf for a special treat. Besides this, people like to receive home-canned goods as a gift, so things like a jelly are fun to give away on special occasions. Canning also provides a measure of security in that you can know that you have extra food available for a hit or miss emergency, whether it is a power failure, a nasty storm, or a national crisis.

This book will guide you in every step you create regarding canning and preserving foods and the way it will result in a good canned product. This guide isn't complicated, for you can do it once you have understood its rules. It will cause you to be curious about canning and preserving foods the way you cannot imagine.

There are lots to think about before proceeding in canning and knowing levels of acidity of foods to understand what method of canning you can do. Knowing also all the required equipment and basic supplies is a step-in guide like mason glass jars, two-piece lids, and bands, large covered water bath or pressure canner, jar lifter, wide-mouth funnel, and a rubber spatula. The canners in the canning process like water bath canners and pressurized canners. It is like going back to basics.

Always put in mind the dos and don'ts in this guide. Make sure to carry out all the proper procedures in canning and preserving. Short cuts aren't allowed, for they are unsafe and may be harmful.

This will guide you to all or any of the items you would like to understand about home canning. It guides you from scratch to a delicious homemade preserve. Self-discipline is required in succeeding in canning. Applying all the proper procedures, tips, and rules in canning will make you a good preserver. You will be able to preserve food anytime without hassles. This guide will enable you to achieve every canning and preserving process you create, so don't be concerned for the best canning and preserving guide is here.

Let's Begin!

Canning Food Basics

It is much easier than you think to can your food. With the growing desire for food that both tastes good and is good for you, now is the time to get started canning at home.

So, let's check out what canning is and why it is a wonderful alternative to purchasing processed food at the grocery.

What is Canning?

A process of preparing food in sealed glass jars in such how that each one the microbes (that cause food to go bad) are destroyed. When canning and sealing properly, a vacuum is made that forestalls more bacteria from growing inside the food.

What about Food Preservation

Food preservations are the processes of preventing food spoilage and wastage. In preserving foods, maintaining nutritional content, texture and flavor are vital. Practicing food preservations prevents the expansion of bacteria, fungi, and other microbes surviving in our food that causes food spoilage and poisoning. Food preservations are the oldest technique in preserving different kinds of food. To survive, we have to find out different techniques for preserving food. This may lessen the food shortage crisis everywhere in the world.

Food preservations are difficult to do as opposed to what others believe, you see that everything that you aren't yet conversant in is hard to do initially, but if you carefully study it, it is extremely simple and easy.

Familiarizing yourself with the various methods of preservations is a great idea. The advantages and drawbacks of preserving food are important to understand also. Knowing the factors like space, climate, equipment, costs, and availability of food are considerably important too. If you recognize all of those facts, you can easily begin preserving food on your own.

Food preservations have been a part of our lives ever since, especially nowadays; the food crisis is getting worst. Food is essential to us; without enough food, you can get weak and, even worst, die. That is why many of us are trying hard to get different sources of food and the way to preserve them. As time goes by, more and more new techniques and ways are being discovered in preserving food for it can save many lives today and for the future generation also.

History Of Canning

The historical backdrop of canning food goes back to 1809

when a French confectioner named Nicolas Francois Appert addressed the test of the French paper Le Monde, who had offered an enormous amount of money to any individual who could imagine a modest and compelling technique for safeguarding a lot of food.

Since tremendous multitudes of men in the Revolutionary War required huge supplies of food day by day, protection was fundamental. Mr. Appert tested and saw that when food was prepared inside a container, it didn't get spoilt except if, indeed, the seal was undermined. He couldn't give the logical purposes for why the food didn't get spoilt, yet the way that it worked was sufficient at that point.

Delicate glass compartments represented a genuine test in the vehicle; they were supplanted with fashioned iron canisters (or, as we as a whole know them, "jars"). Not exclusively can less exorbitant and faster to make. However, they were likewise more secure to move.

The warriors didn't have can openers, so they utilized what they needed to open the jars, which were fundamentally their blades or a stone. The war finished before the canning cycle, and the vehicle of canned food sources was consummated. In 1814, the processing plant Mr. Appert had worked with the prize he got from the challenge was torched by Allied troopers attacking France.

In 1810, a man of his word by the name of Peter Durand protected a cycle of bundling food in fixed impermeable fashioned iron jars by utilizing Appert's strategies, which were at that point set up. Tinned food was costly for conventional individuals to get since it required almost six hours for the food to prepare appropriately on top of the time it took for each can to be hand-made.

In 1812, the primary American canning plant was set up in New York City by Thomas Kensett. He used an improved variant of the created iron jars and safeguarded vegetables, meats, organic products, and clams.

By 1824, meats and stews which were delivered utilizing the strategy found by Mr. Appert were taken to India by Sir William Edward Parry. Tinned food turned into a standing image in Europe among working-class families by then.

By the 1860s, the canning cycle took less time, going from six hours to around thirty minutes. Many canning organizations started to produce in more noteworthy amounts after the wars prompted the nineteenth century. They had the option to offer their canned nourishments to a more extensive crowd moreover.

Because of individuals in Britain during the Victorian period modeling for good-quality food they may store in their storeroom, organizations like Nestle and Heinz went ahead of the scene with great quality tinned nourishment for stores to offer to the working people.

During the first war, military commanders needed large quantities of cheap yet high-calorie food to feed their soldiers. The solution was tinned foodstuffs like bully beef and pork and beans. After the war, the businesses that had supplied the tinned food to the soldiers significantly improved the standard of their goods and thus appealed to the civilian market.

The cans we all know today are made up of tin-coated steel and are used to transport vegetables, meats, fruits, seafood, and a few dairy products.

Why Can Your Food?

It is Healthier!

First and most, canning your homegrown fruits and vegetables gives you control over the chemicals and additives put in your food. You can eat natural, better-tasting food with the confidence that you are not feeding your family something potentially harmful for them.

It Tastes Better!

There is nothing quite like eating your strawberry preserves made with fresh, ripe berries or homemade salsa using tomatoes off the vine in your garden. The store-bought stuff doesn't stand a chance. There is simply no comparison!

— **Make it Your Own!**

Another great reason to can your food is that you can customize it to your preferences.

If you are keen on cinnamon, for instance, you can add it to your apple, peach, or pear jam for a specialty jam only for you. (Feel free to try Spicy Pear Jam... it is one of the most requested jams by my friends and family).

It is Cheaper

Sure, there is an initial investment of some basic canning equipment, but much of it you almost certainly have in your kitchen already. A number of it you can find at a garage and estate sales if you keep your eyes open.

Most of it is re-usable (even the jars), so once you gather the items you may need, your only ongoing expense is going to be new jars (when needed), new jar bands, and the actual ingredients you are going to can.

It Saves Time Later

If you invest a little time now and 'put up' batches of food, you can save time later. You will be more prepared for sudden snowstorms and other unexpected events that may keep you from the store. With a stocked pantry, you are all set!

Getting Prepared For Canning and Preserving

Much the same as a squirrel pressing his home with nuts for the colder time of year, so are home canning lovers getting readied for canning and saving. Indeed, the yields are accessible from your nursery, and in the event that you resemble most, there is an overflow of new leafy foods to manage. So instead of being inefficient, a developing number of people are starting to consider canning and saving food. This is regularly a solid and monetarily stable method of giving elegant dinners to your family all through the on-coming climate months.

So exactly what does one need to do to get readied for the canning of these awesome new food sources? We should follow this simple manual to prepare you to begin your way to fruitful home canning.

Fundamental Preparations for Canning and Preserving

Similarly, as with any undertaking you are going to begin, it generally serves you best to have a strategy in advance. Here are a few things to consider once you are planning to scan and save your new food:

Be Comfortable - wearing the appropriate attire can get things looking great so far.

Encased shoes - it is a smart thought to wear tennis shoes with great help since you will be standing a ton during the canning cycle, which pummels your feet and back. Now and then, the food dribbles and supplies could get dropped; wearing encased shoes will shield your feet from these setbacks.

Covers - a few people like it better to secure their garments with a cover. On the off chance that you have one, wear it.

Shirts and Shorts - this is frequently my undisputed top choice since it is not difficult to move around in this kind of apparel. Remember that whatever you decide to wear, ensure you wouldn't fret about getting it filthy.

Change the A/C down - or acquire an extra fan to the kitchen. It will get hot in there, so attempt to keep yourself somewhat cooler.

Timetable the day for Canning - Canning food takes a touch of your time.

Distribute Time - Don't plan anything on the day you propose to can your food. The planning and handling take up a lot of your chance to wrap up.

Plan your suppers previously - Either set up a dish that will be flown in the broiler or get take out for supper. After every day of canning, you will presumably be drained and not want to cook. However, you and the remainder of your family actually need to eat dinner. Thus, remembering this before you start your canning meeting will facilitate the quandary later.

Prepare the Kitchen - You don't need anything hindering the advancement.

Clean up counters - You will require the space, so don't have anything extra out that will impede your canning.

Clean the ledges - Do a quick disinfectant wipe down before you start canning to ensure the world is without germ.

Void the dishwasher – You will require the dishwasher to scour your containers. After they are done, you can spotless as you come; at that point, fill the dishwasher with the canning supplies you have utilized. This may save the migraine of a wrecking kitchen after the canning project closes.

Assemble Canning and Preserving Supplies – You ought to have all you require accessible before you start.

Containers/Lids/Bands – Make sure you examine the containers for breaks or chips and wash them all together in the dishwasher or hot lathery water. Check the groups for indications of consumption or twists. Supplant with another band if important. Just utilize new canning covers; these aren't securely reusable.

Check your leafy foods - Only utilize flawless new products of the soil for canning. Wash each in cool running water utilizing a vegetable brush to dispose of earth and garbage.

Set up your canning gear - Get the entirety of your canning supplies together for the current venture. Pick your technique for canning. For instance, in the event that the present undertaking is freezing food, at that point, have the entirety of your cooler sacks named and arranged to go. Get out your pots for handling, colanders for depleting, choppers, canning pack, and so on. Remember the little things either like peelers, scrubbers, slashing board, bowls, estimating cups; you get the image.

Canning Equipment

Canning Supplies You Need For Home Canning

The public outcry over the food practices is spurring a renewed interest in home canning...and a good reason! Canning your food at home ensures nothing toxic goes into the food you and your family consume. And it also tastes better!

Try not to let the possibility of canning threaten you. It isn't as hard as you would suspect. You likewise may have to put your life investment funds in beginning a home canning activity in your home. The greater part of the hardware you need you absolutely effectively own. Here is a stock of both the fundamental things just as a couple of different assets you should get as time passes by:

Basics:

Mason Jars

You can regularly discover these glass canning containers at carport deals at sensible costs. Run your finger around the edge of the container (when purchasing used) to ensure you don't feel any chips or marks.

Indeed, even the smallest chip will shield your containers from fixing. Most supermarkets sell containers in different sizes by the case throughout the mid-year and fall canning seasons. (NOTE: Don't utilize reused mayonnaise and other topping containers for canning- - utilize just artisan containers made for the point of canning.)

Seal capable Jar Lids

While you may purchase the containers utilized and re-use them again and again, container tops must be new.

These little metal tops have a rubbery band around them that, when hot, make the seal between the cover and the container. On the off chance that you are purchasing new containers by the case, these tops will be incorporated. On the off chance that you are re-utilizing old containers, the covers are regularly bought independently and are economical.

Jar Bands or Rings

These metal rings screw down on the container to make a comfortable fit between the container and the top. They can be re-utilized and don't should be bought new each time. In the event that you find you are running low on rings, you can take them off cool containers that have just been canned and fixed.

You don't have to store them with the groups screwed on. Once more, on the off chance that you are purchasing new containers by the case, the rings will be remembered for the bundle, yet you can buy them independently moreover.

Boiling Water Canner

This shouldn't be as scary as it sounds...you can utilize a huge stockpot or other enormous, profound saucepot you own. The pot you utilize should be sufficiently enormous to keep the containers you are canning totally lowered (with around 2 inches or a greater amount of water over the container tops) and with sufficient space around the containers that water can move uninhibitedly).

On the off chance that you are utilizing a saucepot from your kitchen, it should have an appropriately fitting top to go with it. You will likewise need to either purchase a wire rack (you can buy them independently in a similar area as the containers in many stores) or make a natively constructed arrangement yourself with the goal that your containers aren't perched on the lower part of the pot unprotected.

An incredible natively constructed arrangement you can utilize is by putting as many containers rings one next to the other on the lower part of the pan as would fit. The containers at that point sit on top of the rings, making space between the pot and the container bottoms.

Kitchen Utensils

Things like estimating cups, wooden spoons (since quite a while ago took care of one work best), scoops, channels, spatulas, and so on

Superfluous items (however accommodating increases):

Jar Lifter

This utensil, like a straightforward contraption, is implied particularly for safe container lifting from bubbling water showers when the containers are excessively hot to the touch. Despite the fact that it isn't significant, it is difficult to can without it (I've utilized customary kitchen utensils previously, which are interesting. The wet containers will, in general, slide from your hold, and to drop a glass container loaded up with bubbling food are a few things you need to evade!)

Lid Lifter

This is a little plastic persevere with a magnet on the base for lifting your container tops out of the quite comfortable water you make them sit in while you are canning. This minuscule lifter is totally NOT fundamental, however modest and very smooth.

Air pocket Remover and be sure secure with the headspace you are leaving; there is no preferable route overestimating it with a uniquely planned gadget to complete the work.

Pressure Canner

This is the most costly speculation of the whole canning measure. However, you can get one for less than $75.00, and it can keep going forever, in any event!

FAQ Home Canning

Here are the four regularly posed inquiries on home canning.

Q. When do I need to utilize a pressing factor canner?

A. A pressing factor canner is required while canning meats and vegetables. On the off chance that you intend to deal with meats and vegetables utilizing the bubbling water canner strategy, you won't have a protected canned item. Pressing factor canners are a lot more secure to utilize these days than in your Grandmother's age. Adhere to the guidelines prior to utilizing, or on the off chance that you are as yet uncertain of the best approach to securely utilize it, think about taking a class.

Q. While canning vegetables, do I need to add salt?

A. No, you don't need to add salt while canning vegetables. The utilization of salt is a private inclination and isn't utilized as an additive.

Q. Do I have to use canning jars?

A. Yes, it is vital that you use jars designed for home canning. They are going to ensure a correct seal by the lids and bands fitting on them correctly. These jars also will withstand the pressure and the heat of a pressure canner. Once you have got proper canning jars, they can be reused year to year. Just remember to examine them for chips and cracks before using any jar.

Q. Do I have to shop for fresh lids each time?

A. Yes, fresh lids are imperative to achieving a good seal. Lids are one piece of canning equipment that you will have to avoid reusing. Canning jars and bands are often reused each canning season, but lids cannot.

Q. Which jars are recommended for Home Canning, and which of them should I avoid?

A. You will have to use jars that are specifically made for canning.

Jars made of the Jarden Company, like name brands of Ball, Kerr, and Mason, are excellent canning jars. These jars are specially made for home canning and can give you the best results when using the right bands and brand-new lids.

Before you use a canning jar, you will need to scrub it with hot, soapy water. Then, you will need to examine the rim of the jar to make sure it has no cracks or chips.

One of the most reasons that a jar doesn't seal after it is has gone through the home canning process is that non-canning jars were used. Many of us think that if a band fits on the top of a glass jar that it is often used for canning, but this is often incorrect. It is going to appear to suit the threads, but it is not going to really fit properly.

You want to avoid using glass jars that are designed for one-time-only use. These are commercial jars that you may buy food in from the grocery like mayonnaise, jelly, pasta sauce, or the other food that is sold in glass jars.

The correct canning supplies are vital when home canning. You will have to shop for jars that are specifically designed for home canning. There is no sense spending all of your time and energy canning only to have the seal fail due to using non-canning jars.

Dos and Don'ts For Home Canning

There is an upswing in additional people starting to can and preserve food. It stands with good reason.

Canning your food is a good way to save lots of money in these tough economic times, which isn't looking to do just that.

What a lot of beginners need to know is that there are certain Dos and Don'ts for Home Canning that are imperative to securely preserve food. Keeping that in mind, here is a list of the most common things to think about once you are canning and preserving food at home.

Dos and Don'ts for Home Canning Safety

Dos

Start with good quality fresh fruits and vegetables that are thoroughly rinsed and scrubbed with a vegetable brush to get rid of debris.

Only use glass home canning jars (mason/Kerr jars) with 2-part sealing lids and bands.

Prepare the lids and jars according to the manufacturer's suggestions.

Choose the acceptable canning method for the foods being preserved.

Have all of your canning utensils available and prepared to use before you start preserving food.

Make sure to examine the canning jars for chips or cracks as this will affect whether the jars seal properly as well as add a risk of breakage during the canning process.

Wash and sterilize the canning jars.

Allow for proper headspace when filling the jars.

Follow the canning recipes exactly.

Stick to recommended processing times for every canning project.

Store canned foods in a cool, dry, and dark place.

Don'ts

Don't forget to scrub your hands before you begin your canning project. Sash up again in the canning process if you sneeze or need to use the toilet.

Do not use "commercial" jars like spaghetti or mayo jars. They are not meant for canning and carry a high risk of breakage during the canning process.

Only use a 2-piece band and lid set for sealing jars. Bands could also be used again and again as long as they are not rusted or bent. Never reuse a canning lid; once it is used, it will not be able to reseal during processing.

Don't use the open kettle or any sort of oven method for preserving and canning. The USDA and other authority sites have stated that this is often not a secure way to can food.

Don't overtighten bands

Don't deviate from canning recipes; they are measured out to make sure that the food will stay safe and process correctly.

Hot liquids in cold jars don't mix; make sure your jars are heated before filling them to avoid breakage.

Don't forget to label the canned foods with their content and date of processing.

Don't store jars the wrong way up once processed.

Don't under process the foods being canned.

Don't remove the lid to the canning pot while the processing goes on.

Don't plan to eat any canned foods that appear to have not been sealed properly and have mold or discoloration.

Steps For Water Bath Canning

Water shower canning is the way toward murdering hurtful microorganisms through bubbling. This technique is furthermore referenced as the bubbling water strategy; it is supposed to be the most straightforward and most ideal path for saving high corrosive food sources. It wrecks any dynamic microscopic organisms and microorganisms in your food that makes it protected to be utilized sometime in the future.

High corrosive products of the soil are reasonable for water shower canning on the grounds that the vast majority of these microorganisms in high corrosive food sources are executed even through bubbling as it were. In this cycle, a temperature of 100 degrees Centigrade should be kept up to slaughter these microorganisms.

Most canned food sources like jams, jams, savors, pickles, rations, jelly, preserves, and fermented tomatoes are prepared submerged in shower canning. Handling shower canning isn't muddled and hard.

You can do it with your family too. All techniques in water shower canning are extremely basic and clear to follow.

That is the reason the vast majority utilize this canning strategy hence. Center and consistently recollect the significant subtleties in canning, and obviously, you will accomplish your canning cycle.

The tips, rules, materials, and safeguards in water canning are straightforward.

There aren't leads hard to follow on the off chance that you have self-control in yourself. Following these significant subtleties in canning will end in great quality canned nourishments. Here are basic bit by bit methodology in water shower canning;

1. Organize instruments and gear.
2. Fill your water canner with 66% loaded up with water

than heat.

3. Dunk canning containers and tops in steaming hot water.

4. Move arranged nourishments into the new canning containers and remove air rises with an elastic spatula.

5. Wipe the canning container edges with a spotless fabric.

6. Spot cover onto each container and hand-fix the groups.

7. Orchestrate the rack inside your water shower canner and place filled containers in the rack; at that point, lower it into heated water.

8. Cover and stand by till water bubbles, decreasing warmth and looking after the bubble.

9. After the time span, eliminate containers from the canner with a container lifter and permit them to cool.

10. Test the seals on containers by pushing the center of the cover.

11. Name canning containers like the date prepared and substance, and store them in a cool, dull, and dry spot. Water shower canning is ideal to do at home and ought to be a decent kind of revenue as well.

Mistakes You Can Prevent

Canning isn't complicated, neither is it scary, even when pressure canners sometimes make strange whistling sounds. The method is kind of simple. Anyone can successfully pull it off as long as standard procedures are followed and canning mistakes are prevented. Follow USDA recommendations and guidelines, and listen to the recommendation of master canning experts. Their knowledge is effective. It can prevent a lot of your time wasted on experiments.

10 Common Canning Mistakes

They are selecting the incorrect canner - Recipes mention which type of canner to use. Water bath and pressure canners aren't interchangeable. Use a water bath canner for acidic foods like tomatoes, fruit, pickles, and sweet preserves. Non-acidic foods like plain vegetables, meat, soups, and broth must be preserved using a pressure canner.

Dirty jar rims - a little fluff can prevent lids from sealing. Even if jars feel closed, the lids will loosen soon thereafter, and the food inside will spoil.

Ignoring altitude - Do you live more than 1000 feet above sea level? Adjust canning time, whether you pressure can or use the water bath method. Water boils at a special temperature at higher altitudes than it does at the stumped level.

Overfilling jars - Follow canning recipes. When you overfill jars, their content will boil over during the canning process. The lids will fail to seal. Don't forget to stir the jar content before putting it on lids. Air bubbles got to be released.

Changing the recipe - One of the most common canning mistakes is deviating from recommended recipes. For example, adding extra flour, starch, or other thickening agents slows down the speed of heat penetration. This leads to under-cooking. You can always thicken your products at the time of consumption.

Using poor ingredients - Choose the best possible ingredients for canning if you would like tasty food. Select the freshest vegetables, preferably from your garden.

Reusing lids - The ring of adhesive on traditional canning lids wears out when reused. The jars won't seal. Tattler reusable canning lids are the exception.

Using broken jars - Inspect jars and lids before every usage. A hairline crack in glass can have devastating results. It is quite messy when a jar breaks inside a canner. Sterilize all equipment thoroughly before every usage. Only use jars made for canning. Mayonnaise jars won't work because the glass is just too thin.

Skimping on the water - The jars placed during a water bath canner got to be covered with at least one or two inches of water. This ensures that the food is heated evenly from all sides.

Moving warm jars - Select a spot on your kitchen counter you do not need for a couple of hours. Jars should cool undisturbed. They will unseal whenever the recent food hits the adhesive seal of the lids.

Reasons Why You Can't Afford To Not

"Canning is simply excessively costly!" "Who has the opportunity to can?" "For what reason should I can when I can hurry to the shop and purchase in at a bargain?" I've heard these articulations and others consistently. While genuine that canning requires a level of your time and energy, it very well may be amazingly fulfilling.

Additionally, canning requires an underlying cost of cash for containers, covers, and produce. Be that as it may, the points of interest far exceed the costs caused. There are 3 reasons why you, in a real sense, can't bear to not can!

1. "Forgetting healthy, the kind of food you eat is everything."

Did you realize that most of all, ailment and sickness are straightforwardly connected to abstain from food? As the colloquialism goes, "the type of food you eat will affect your general health." Furthermore, a significant part of the food we eat is bound artificially, substantial metals, poisons, and other malignancy causing specialists. These synthetic compounds incorporate MSG (an additive), aspartame (soda pop sugar), and a whole host of shading specialists, colors, and things that can't be articulated! Studies have demonstrated MSG to be found in 70% of every prepared food. MSG has been connected to corpulence, diabetes, headache, cerebral pains, chemical imbalance, ADHD, and even Alzheimer's! Additionally, hereditarily changed food presently contains a lot of our food sources too.

Aspartame and GM food are truly downright awful in most countries aside from the United States! They look at aspartame as a toxic substance! With the multiplication of those dangerous added substances which are immersing our food supply, is anyone shocked there is a particularly uncontrolled expansion in infections? Notwithstanding, by canning, you can be guaranteed that you and your family approach the most perfect and most life-upgrading nourishments accessible. You, in a real sense, realize what went into the container!

2. "It costs what amount?"

The expense of food is rising quickly. Studies show an ascent in certain nourishments by as much as 2-3 times what they weren't path back. The US Department of Labor indicated an ascent in milk, eggs, bread, flour, and other "basics" by up to 40% from 2016 to 2017.

In any case, these insights don't contemplate swelling, which has risen alarmingly. By canning, you acquire a proportion of power over these cost increments. Canning is a functional and sound judgment approach for the present or the upcoming monetary vulnerabilities. The brilliant thing is, by canning, you are making sure about the upcoming food at the present costs!

3. "Where's the hamburger?"

Food deficiencies are currently approaching on the overall skyline. Regardless of whether you can manage the cost of the increasing expense of food presently, will you have the option to later? Wheat supplies worldwide have tumbled to 30-year lows. USA stores have tumbled to a stunning long term low! Because of the biofuel business, interest in corn is surpassing stockpiles. This progressively influences the cereals and grain supplies.

This result is unfavorably influencing the meat and dairy ventures - which definitely is driving the value for these items through the rooftop. Couple this with serious dry spell and climate marvels presently being knowledgeable about a significant part of the world, and you have the elements for deficiencies. How might this affect you and your family? It intends to make a move! By canning, you not just have the best food accessible and the most financially savvy - yet in addition, you have food to supply for yourself and your friends and family.

Water Bath Canning Vs. Pressure Canning

While picking the best approach to pickle or what pickle plans you'd wish to attempt, there are an assortment of things you need to remember. Something or other is which canning strategy you'd wish to utilize. Home canning is a straightforward cycle that should be possible to pressure canning or water-shower canning. Pressing factor canning is a cycle that needs a pressing factor canner, which may frequently be costly.

You may be that as it may, have the option to locate a cheap one with a smidgen of chasing through carport deals or swap meets. Water-shower canning, then again, is regularly done utilizing a couple of simple instruments. We will accept that you will be utilizing a water-shower canning technique. The accompanying will clarify this specific technique.

First and foremost, truth be told, you may require a water-shower canner. You need to ensure it is sufficiently profound to convey enough water to lower your canning containers by, in any event, 1 inch. You will likewise require your canning containers, screw-on groups, and canning tops. It is a considerably less-costly, reliable method of canning. It is a method of saving numerous food sources, including salsa, jam, jam, salted organic products, and vegetables, likewise as a relish for a long time. It is an amazing canning technique for amateurs or ardent canners.

A water-shower canner is basically an outsized pot with a rack that will postpone to seven bricklayer quart containers or up to sixteen-16 ounces containers. By utilizing a huge stockpot and being innovative with wire, one could ad-lib a rack to make their water shower canner. However long the containers evade direct warmth from the burner and are totally lowered in the water, an assortment of cunning arrangements may be utilized. On the off chance that you'd wish to save the trouble of gear your own, they will be promptly bought at numerous areas or on the web.

The way water-shower canner capacities is that it builds the temperature of your canning container to a temperature sufficiently hot to slaughter yeast, microbes, and molds that are found in food. The warmth likewise makes air bubbles that push the air inside the container out in light of the fact that the substance inside the container warm and extends. At the point when the container chills directly off to temperature, the air pressure makes a seal that thwarts air and different life forms from entering the container, keeping the food from ruining, in this manner, the purpose behind canning's presence.

The containers should be liberated from scratches or breaks in which the edge is level. They should be recently washed, either by hand or dishwasher, with the goal that they are sterile and liberated from any miniature living beings. The strategy starts by filling the canning container with the predetermined fixings. Try to clean the edge off with a washed towel so on make an ideal seal.

Spot the cover on edge, guaranteeing to focus it with the goal that the elastic is all in all edge; at that point, screw on the band. The band shouldn't be in a bad way on firmly; over-fixed groups don't permit the gasses to escape the containers. At that point, you can put the containers into the water-shower on the rack.

Ensure the water is covering the entirety of the containers by at any rate one inch; at that point, heat the water to the point of boiling. At the point when completed, turn off the warmth and let sit for an entire five minutes prior to eliminating containers from the canner. Make a point to let the canning containers cool, not to consume yourself.

As the canning containers chill, the tops should pop shut as they seal, implying that; subsequent to fixing, the tops won't push down by pushing down with your finger. In the event that the containers aren't fixed, the center of the cover will manifest and down when squeezed. Either discard these containers or eat the substance in seven days. On the off chance that the covers didn't seal, don't utilize them again as they are going to not seal whenever utilized once more.

When the containers are cooled, they will be put away. It is ideal in the event that they are put away in a cool, dull spot, sort of a cellar or washroom. The substance will be prepared to eat as per the formula. Ensure that prior to eating, the substance is reviewed for indications of waste: form, gas, shadiness, scents, or seepage. In the event that decay has happened, don't eat the substance of the can in light of the fact that it might cause genuine disease.

Here is a straightforward pickling formula for you to test!

Delightful Pickles:

- Wash cucumbers, pack them into sanitized canning containers.
- Solution (adequate for 3 gallons of pickles in glass containers):
- 1-gallon of vinegar
- 1 cup of salt

½ pound (16 tablespoons) of powdered mustard, try to totally blend the powdered mustard in with vinegar so that there are no bunches. A decent method to do that is to take a little vinegar and make a glue sort of substance with the powdered mustard; at that point, blend this into the vinegar. Pour blend over cucumbers in your sanitized containers and seal straightforwardly (Using the strategy of your decision.)—store pickles without eliminating screw groups.

Importance of Using Labels

Canning Labels are an important part of any home canner's tools. While using labels is a sure way to improving your home canning experience, there are several ways to label your canned food.

The best way to label your canning is to write it down on the jar lid with a sharpie. Some manufacturers make canning lids that have lines printed on the lid expressly for labeling purposes. While this is often a fast and dirty method, it is not very visually pleasing. It also presents a serious problem. After you consume the contents of the jar, the lid remains labeled for old food and is difficult to reuse. If you desire a neater, more professional-looking way to label your canning, you can use stick-on labels.

Stick-on labels are available in two forms, those made to be attached to the lid of the jar and people meant to be attached to the jar itself. A good type of both forms of labels exists for do-it-your-selfers to use. Buying stick-on labels at the local office supply store are one solution. Unfortunately, these labels aren't designed specifically for canning and cannot be very durable.

Some websites offer canning specific labels that you can download and print at home. These labels are going to be designed to contain important canning information like date, contents, and batch number but will still need to be printed on weak material.

The best solution is to order canning specific labels online. You can be ready to get the widest range of colors and styles and sturdy labels. These sites have waterproof labels, which is vital because canning involves water baths.

Although there is a good kind of labeling solution, some sort of labeling can be used for multiple reasons. One must label the contents, date canned, batch number, and the canner's name.

Labeling the contents of the jar could seem simple but is extremely important. For instance, there are many types of jams or pickles, and it is going to be hard to spot what type of blueberry jam is in a particular jar. Additionally, if you propose to give your canning as a present to family and friends, it will not be as easy for them to spot what is in a certain jar.

The date is one of the most important things to label on your canning jars. The date is vital because you can remember when you can have a favorite food and can plan your future canning projects when the food is the freshest. Labeling the date also prevents you from eating very old jars that will be lurking in your pantry for years. It also assists in moving older jars to the front of your pantry so that they are eaten first and prevents spoilage.

The batch number is a simple way for you to manage spoilage if it does occur. When you can large amounts of food, you create several runs in your canner. If a specific jar goes bad too soon, you can easily identify what batch it had been from check the condition of other jars from that specific batch.

Canning labels are important tools for home preservers and will always be used. They are going to improve the design of your canning jars, assist you in remembering what is in the jars and the date they were canned.

Food Preservation Techniques

Restaurants worldwide use various techniques to preserve food, counting on factors just like the ingredient, the climate, taste required, etc. Our ancestors have used various preservation techniques like canning, drying, pickling, and lots of more, which are still getting used in today's times. Let's have a sneak peek at the top 10 food preservation techniques starting from ancient methods to the modern day of food preservation.

Ancient techniques- There are various ancient techniques that are still useful in today's world. Food preservation of the olden times most ordinarily used salt, oil, sugar, among many other basic ingredients for preservation. It is also very often said that these methods preserve food longer as compared to present-day techniques.

Drying- Drying is a technique carried from the traditional times till now, and it involves removing the moisture from the food until there is no moisture enough to breed microbes. It is mostly finished preserving certain vegetables, fruits, meats, and lots more. It is often done with various methods starting from simple to using heavy equipment.

Fermenting- This method involves producing 'good bacteria' to inhibit the 'bad bacteria' from breeding. Fermenting is typically done on fruits (like grapes to supply wine), meat (like cured sausage), dairy products (like producing yoghurt). Although the tactic seems easy, it involves paying attention at different levels for various products.

Pickling- Pickling involves soaking meat, vegetables, or fruits and the likes in a solution made from oils, salt, acid, etc. Pickling is often tedious because it involves making the answer in the right concentration also taking excellent care of the merchandise once it is pickled. This method is typically combined with other methods like fermenting, canning, or refrigerating, as pickling alone might not work out.

Dry salting- This method involves covering food in a very high concentration of salt. This method is one of the earliest kinds of food preservation and is additionally considered tastier and fresher in comparison to canning. Salted vegetables and meat were highly used during the 20th century.

Cellaring- This method is additionally one of the earliest forms of preserving wherein the food is stored under specific conditions like high humidity and a light-controlled space. Many grains, nuts, vegetables, etc., are stored in this way across the world. It is also one of the simplest methods of preservation.

Although there are many ancient techniques used in food preservation, hotels lately prefer the modern and easier techniques.

Refrigeration and freezing- This is often the most commonly used among the top 10 food preservation techniques. Refrigeration helps in slowing down the method of bacterial breeding, while freezing helps in completely canceling the method. Most sorts of foods are frozen except fruits, unless for specific requirements or recipes.

Freeze drying- Freeze drying is far more intense than normal freezing and doesn't affect the taste intrinsically. This system helps in removing the moisture completely from the food by turning it into ice first, then into vapor. This is often widely used in making instant coffee.

Carbonated water- This method is typically used for the preservation of carbonated drinks, as the name suggests. Soda water is nothing but CO_2 dissolved in water under pressure. The oxygen is totally eliminated from the water in order that no microbial growth is inspired.

Chemical food preservation- this is often the most common method of food preservation and is additionally considered unhealthy to a particular extent. Even though it is widely practiced because it is far more economical and it also helps in preserving the food longer. Chemical preserves either eliminate or slow down bacterial activity or function as antioxidants.

Food irradiation- This is often one of the newest methods of food preservation, and it uses gamma-ray to kill bacteria. Food in packets is typically nuclear radiated then sealed airtight. However, this method isn't widely practiced due to its expense.

Although new methods of preservation are arising, only a few countries have adopted them.

Preserving Fruits The Proper Way

Keeping fruits fresh for a long period isn't difficult if correct preservation techniques are applied. So, before we start, certain things like pectin powder/ liquid, lemon juice, sugar, vitamin C, any artificial sweetener, glass/ plastic freezer containers are needed first.

Over a span of your time, fruits tend to darken. To stop this, it is good to coat them with acidic juice like the juice of lemon, orange, or pineapple. There are commercial anti-darkening products available in the market that will be used. Soaking the fruits in vitamin C also will prevent them from darkening over a long period of your time.

If you do not wish to coat or soak fruits in preservatives, you can alternatively use glass or plastic freezer containers. These are special containers that will keep fruits in good quality under freezing conditions.

Fruits like apples, figs, plum, mulberry, cherry, peach, blackberry, and grapes taste great as jams and jellies. So, if you wish to have these fruits in the form of jellies, then preserving becomes a lot easier. Just prepare the jelly and preserve it in a glass container.

Drying fruits is additionally a good way of preserving them. People wish to consume some fruits in dried condition. Often fruits like apples, pears, and plums are dried and preserved. A food dehydrator is often used to dry the fruits in the form of slices. These dried fruits are stored in airtight containers.

Pint or quart jars also can be used for preserving fruits. Fruits are often hot packed by adding it in raw condition to a hot syrup then reheating it to boiling point. This could then be packed in the containers along with the syrup.

The canning of fruits is additionally a good method of preservation. Cut fruit into half and take away the core and stem. This will give you two edible halves. You can slice the fruit the way you wish. The slices are then heat processed and sealed in airtight containers.

Fruits should be consumed once they are fresh and ripe. However, if you wish to consume it after some time, the above-mentioned tips should assist you in preserving your favorite fruits for an extended time.

Strawberries

Canning strawberries as a whole and intact fruit are nearly impossible because the fruit is very soft and has very high water content. The same is true when it involves freezing them. The best method so far is to preserve them as jam then can this. You can do that carefully and in a way that can keep the fruit as a whole as possible.

It is not impossible to achieve success when canning strawberries, but you will probably discover that they are going to lose some of the flavor and some of their colors as a result of the method. This may vary between varieties, and other people are always trying to find out the most suitable variety for successful canning.

Can the fruit in the usual way using rapid processing in a rotary cooker for the best results or 6 - 10 minutes at 100 degrees centigrade in other cookers? Follow this with thorough and fast cooling. After canning strawberries, cover the jars with paper to keep the light out. This may improve the time. These can then be used for creating desserts or maybe eating as they are. They are exquisite with waffles!

Strawberry jam is a lovely way of preserving and canning strawberries and can be used for desserts, also like bread, waffles, or scones. It is also used with cream as a sandwich filling for sponge cakes. It is best to use pectin for creating strawberry preserves to make sure that it sets to a good consistency. The best pectin is to use is the 'low sugar' or maybe 'no sugar' varieties as these will provides a stronger strawberry flavor to your preserve.

Many strawberry preserves recipes suggest that you mash the fruit. This is often a matter of choice, and a few people will like better to find whole strawberries in the jar.

If you mash the fruit, you will probably find yourself with a thicker consistency, but I do think that it is lovely to find some whole fruit when preserving or canning strawberries. I really like it when you are lucky enough to seek out an entire strawberry appear on a scone; it is a bit like winning at the lucky dip!

Do not feel that you need to stick rigidly to the recipe when it involves the quantity of sugar that you add.

Try the strawberries first, and if you think that they are quite sharp, then you may wish to add a little more sugar. Likewise, if you prefer a pointy strawberry flavor, you can reduce the measurement slightly. The flavor of the fruit can vary tremendously from variety to variety and also counting on where and once they were picked.

Whatever your choice of preserving, making jam or canning strawberries is a wonderful way to keep a little taste of summer for those dark and cold winter tea times.

Tomatoes

Deciding the way to preserve tomatoes you have grown in your garden will depend upon how you would like to use them in the future and what kind of space you have to store them. Typically, you can either dehydrate or can tomatoes, and clearly, dehydration will take up less space. Canning can take up more room with many jars to be stored, but canning also offers more variety in the ways you can preserve tomatoes.

If you choose to dehydrate them, you can use a machine or allow them to dry on their own in the sun. Who hasn't heard of sun-dried tomatoes? With dehydration, you can also preseason them before they are dehydrated, or you can leave them natural. Seasoned sun-dried tomatoes and be added to several dishes, including salads. Dried tomatoes are often used for soups and reconstituted for other uses.

The dehydrated tomato has generally not been cooked; it is preserved in its unpeeled, raw state. The keys are air and heat, and the tomato should be thinly sliced. The standard equipment used for dehydrating is a machine, an oven, or in the sun.

If you use the sun to dry them, make sure they are covered to keep the insects and dirt far away from them as they dry. This method takes the longest and can take a couple of days of putting them in the sun every day and bringing them in the dark. Whatever method you use, make sure they are completely dry, or they are going to mold.

If canning tomatoes is the route you want, you can also make various kinds of tomato products to be used. They will be crushed, diced, whole, pureed, and made into paste, sauce, soup, salsa, ketchup, and juice. They will be peeled or unpeeled, and appropriate seasonings added to get the specified outcome; for instance, salsa gets different seasonings than pasta sauce. As in the case of salsa, tomatoes are often combined with other foods like onions and peppers.

When canning tomatoes, they are always cooked. The canning process cooks them. The key to canning is the removal of microorganisms and an airtight environment. The common equipment for canning is either a water bath canner or a pressure canner. Since tomatoes have a high acid level, they will be safely preserved using a water bath canner. Special jars and lids are needed to carry the tomatoes for preservation, and a couple of other items like a rack and tongs for handling hot jars are necessary.

Tomatoes are a really versatile food, and knowing the way to preserve tomatoes will assist you in keeping your pantry filled with what you wish to eat.

Cabbage

A great many people are familiar with canning food. Sooner or later in their life, they have attempted canned food sources, arranged canned food sources themselves, or watched somebody really do it. You can take practically any vegetable, organic product, and a couple of sorts of meat and can them. A top pick of mine turns out to can a cabbage. One thing you need to recall while canning cabbage, alongside the other food thing, is the thing that year your formula came from.

Plans for canning cabbage, and the other nourishment so far as that is concerned, ought to be in a book no more seasoned than 10 years in light of the fact that a ton of rules and guidelines are changed in 10 years and to stay up to speed and adapt to everything, your smartest choice for canning cabbage from a formula is the fresher, the better.

Likewise, another tip while canning cabbage is you may have to take a situation in canning cabbage plans. The canning cabbage plans permit individuals to discover more current and better approaches to make food. The canning cabbage plans additionally give various measures of container creation, so relying on the number of containers you might want to supply will all rely on the formula you follow.

Additionally, while canning nourishments, you will see certain food sources require somewhat more vinegar than others because of the corrosive levels not being fitting. Corrosive likewise alluded to as vinegar, adds to the food protection measure. It is the key fixing that permits the food to stay useful for long after it is readied. Another great reality a few people that probably won't be familiar with canning should know is that you can utilize two distinct kinds of canners all the while. You can utilize a water shower canner, which might be somewhat obsolete. The water shower canner was what our folks and grandparents utilized years back while canning food. In any case, it actually completes the work, and the food tastes as incredible as the other canner could permit. The steam canner is the one that I like, however. With the steam canner, you utilize 3 pints of water, which is a path not exactly what the water shower scanner requires.

The marvelous thing about utilizing less water is your water bill will be brought down in cost than if you were utilizing the water shower canner. By utilizing less water, you are additionally assisting the climate, which prompted the whole "practicing environmental safety" rage is going better than anyone might have expected. We might want to make ourselves as well as other people aware of the dangers once we as a general public become too inefficient and a steam canner diminishes our waste levels. Additionally, a steam canner is prepared to warm up in a fraction of the time as a water shower canner takes.

By warming up quicker, the canner is in a situation to supply more containers of food at a quicker speed, which is amazingly helpful for the person. On the off chance that there are any inquiries you have that can't be found in a formula book, you can look through the web, and you will discover everything without exception you have inquiries on.

Hot peppers formula

The flavor of this formula is it relies upon if you need it more sizzling. At that point, on the off chance that you understand what you need, it is dependent upon you to add additional fixings like bean stew powder or whatever fixings you wish. Above all and principal, there are numerous things that you should know and be helped to remember, much the same as the things that are utilized in canning like a pressing factor canner (12 qt. limit or more), canning containers and new covers, and rings, a container lifter that is utilized for pulling the new containers in the wake of preparing, and a canning pipe. What's more, in the event that you have the entirety of the things in you, at that point, you would now be able to begin doing the formula.

In setting up the canning hot peppers formula, you need the accompanying fixings like 5 pounds of ground meat, 2 cups of cleaved onions, 1 clove of squashed garlic, 6 cups of canned tomatoes and juice, one cup of bean stew powder, 1 tbsp. of salt, 1 hot red pepper, hacked daintily, and 1 tsp. Of ground cumin. These are the ensuing fixings that are required in making a hot pepper formula.

The fixings that are recorded above are frequently changing whether you incline toward adding a few additional cloves of garlic and another hot pepper. However, it relies on how hot the peppers are or what completes one enjoys most. What's more, some of the time, you can likewise add one cup of vinegar and a great deal of ketchup utilizing tablespoons and utilize 2 tsp of cumin rather for enhancing. By adding additional fixings, it causes a piece to be hot.

Directions for canning hot peppers formula as follows:

1. At the lower part of a huge pot, the base meat, onions, and garlic ought to be cook until earthy colored. It ought to be depleted with the goal that the amount of fat will reduce. So that high fat can't be remembered for jars since it tends to cause a greater extent of container seals, which is the reason it fizzles during handling.

2. Add the excess fixings and diminish the warmth when it bubbles. Keep cooking for around 20 minutes. Eliminate the drifting fat.

3. Meanwhile, set up a pressing factor canner with various creeps of bubbling water. Spot clean containers in the bubbling water or it is regularly washed in a dishwasher; however, on the off chance that solitary your dishwasher has a Sani-cycle, it is better.

4. Spot the container covers in steaming hot water and prepare them when you are to utilize them.

5. Top off the new containers individually; they ought to have in any event 1 inch of headspace. Headspace is the amt. of space between the top and the bean stew.

Eliminate air rises from the combination, assuming any, utilizing a plastic blade or either a straw or is frequently a plastic bubbler that is accessible from Ball.

6. Clean the edges of the containers with a dry towel, so they are completely spotless for them to be fixed well. Put the cover on and press the ring until the motivation behind the obstruction is met. Spot the container into the bubbling water inside the canner, and still top off the leftover containers until all are utilized.

7. Spot the top on the canner yet leave the tap open, or in the event that you are utilizing a weighted check canner, don't put the heap on for 10 min. It is important to vent a pressing factor canner so that there are no air pockets in the canner during preparation; after 10 min. of venting, close the tap or position the weighted measure. Try not to begin timing until the measure starts to shake 2-3 times a min, or on the off chance that you are utilizing a dial check canner when the pressing factor comes up to 10 lbs.

8. Begin timing. Handling of half quart containers is for 60 minutes—15 min. or then again qt. Containers are for 60 minutes. 30 min. Long. In the event that you are at a preferred height over 2000 feet, check your USDA augmentation about changing handling times for the rise.

9. At the point when the time span has finished, let the pressing factor canner chill for at least 30 min. Also, eliminate the stacking check. After the pressing factor is at 0 pounds psi or (on dial check, or not steam escapes after the heap is taken out), at that point, it is the protected chance to dispose of the top. Face the top far

away from you as it is eliminated. Be cautious about the steam.

Allow containers to sit for in any event 5 min. in the canner, at that point eliminate utilizing the container lifter to a without draft spot to chill and leave it for at any rate 24 hrs. At that point, eliminate the rings and wash containers. Test the covers by tapping tenderly with a metal spoon. You will hear a ringing sound. What's more, in the event that you hear a dull sound from a container that doesn't sound much the same as the other, break the seal and put the container in the fridge and use in a few days or reprocess it in 24 hrs. Another cover ought to be utilized.

Lemons

When you are processing lemons or limes, it pays to use a high-grade citrus juicer rather than your hands or the lightweight plastic cup and cone juicers found in many kitchens. Using a citrus juicer can save a lot of time if you are preserving your own fruit, as the only easiest method to save lots of your fruit crush for later use is to freeze it. If you have a surplus of lemons or limes, you can choose to preserve them by several methods. You can use a pressure canner or bottler to keep chunks of fruit in syrup.

To do this, you need a pressure canning set, but it is a cheap way to store a lot of fruit for a long time (several years if you do everything by the books). However, not everyone has the equipment, and buying it is only worthwhile if you propose to create a lot of preserves per annum.

You can also pickle lemons in a sweet sugar and vinegar solution. This tastes quite nice and is usually used in Asian cuisine. Pickling really only requires vinegar, spices, and your fruit and is wiped out old jam or spread jars, so it is fairly cheap. The best way to preserve is just freezing, though, as you can get by with minimal processing.

It does require a little freezer space, but if you have this, then it is a good option. Whole fruit generally doesn't keep well, going mushy and gray when defrosted.

The best thing to do is to squeeze the juice, then freeze this in whatever size you are likely to use it in. for instance, use takeaway food containers for giant batches for lemonade, or use cube trays if all you use is little amounts in cooking or baking.

Green Beans

Canning fresh green beans are extremely easy to do, provided you have the proper equipment. Here is a list of what you may need to scan your fresh beans.

1. Fresh Green Beans, now anyone that has grown beans knows how well they produce during the summer months, so quit giving them away and begin canning them.

2. You will need canning jars. I always recommend Ball canning jars or Kerr Canning jars,

3. A good pressure cooker is important with any type of home canning, an excellent place to get one is at an area ironmongery shop that is indecently owned. You may ask yourself, well, why not go to w mart or some superstore? The answer is easy. The people at your local ironmongery shop can answer any questions you will have, and I promise you will not get that at any

supermarket.

4. Canning Salt, which is bought at almost any supermarket.

5. Lids and Rings, Lids can't be used from year to year, but however, you can reuse the rings (that is, the screw on the part of the jar).

6. A good source of heat, I do all my canning outdoors (as it can get extremely hot in the summer, I do not heat up the house, I do it in the garage). I also use a propane burner as a source of heat.

Well, that is about all you will need, so here is how we prepare the fresh green beans. Wash, wash, and wash again. This is vital. I rinse my fresh green beans in cold water several times, no need to dry them as they are going to get fully cooked in the canning process. Cut or break your fresh green beans into bite-size pieces, a little over an inch long.

Now you are ready to pack them in the canning jars. Take the canning jars and place about one teaspoon of canning salt in the bottom, pack the canning jar filled with beans, fill the jar with water up to about 3/4 from the top, now place on the lid and screw the cap on (do not over tighten).

Now you are ready to process the beans in your pressure cooker, this is often where some people get a bit scared, but not to worry. Place the filled canning jars in the bottom of the cooker and fill with cold water up to about 1 inch from the top of the jars; now secure the lid to the top of your canner and lightweight the propane burner. Grab a cool drink, and once the steam starts to come out of the petcock, place it on the small pressure flipper. Keep your head steady and what you want is to take care of 15 pounds of pressure for about 15 minutes; this is often a pint-size recipe only, so if you do quarts, consult your canner directions. Store your canned green beans in a cool dark place, and they will stay for several months.

Benefits Derived From Canning And Preserving Food

There is much that will be said about storing foods and preserving them in the manner used by our ancestors. Traditional methods of food preservation have slowly been fading from our modern life, and it is essential to recollect that when these routines are gone, they are going to be lost forever. It is left to our own devices to find out and to perpetuate these traditions revolving around canning, freezing, drying, or smoking for the advantages of our grandchildren and for his or her children also.

Our life would undoubtedly be boring if we were to follow the precise habits of our forefathers and merely consumed that which was currently in season. It is imperative that we reflect upon the processes of preserving food to allocate some variety into our daily menu selection.

We could very easily exit our door and leap into the front seat of our car and hastily make our way to the local grocery to fetch several cans of corn or to go to the frozen foods department for a medium bag of spinach to finish the evening meal but would you not feel better reaching into your home pantry shelf and taking out a quart jar of this or of that?

The foods which we will or preserve by any accepted method has specific benefits related to them. We can rest assured that the efforts which we place into preserving these foods aren't wasted but will provide a needed benefit to ourselves and to our families. Let's briefly review several of those benefits at this point.

The first entry that I might wish to cover involves the environmental. With increased frequency, many of my fellow Americans are getting truly concerned about the damage placed upon the environment by mankind. These impairments are usually non-reversible and can often bequeath our future generations with a deficit of valuable resources. By using the principles presented for food preservation, we can reduce this undesirable footprint greatly.

Local farmer's markets are arising all across the state as more and more city people are starting to realize the benefits of buying locally produced vegetables and fruits. This return to locally grown produce has evolved into a new name for those that support such a venture, they are affectionately referred to as "Locavores," and most of those people would now like better to consume the foods grown in their specific area as against importing them from across the state. Not only does this policy instill a boost towards environmental concerns, but the provisions obtained will retain its flavor and taste far better at the end of the day.

For many of us, keeping the tradition alive is a crucial step towards leaving something to future generations of a family. Although they might easily rush to the grocery for his or her needs, they might prefer the old fashion method of "doing it themselves." These moments provide inspirations of great pride and represent cherished moments for bonding with relations, which ultimately generate wonderful memories to look back upon in future years.

Of all the advantages attributed to preserving food at home, we cannot overlook the advantage of enjoying freshly preserved produce or the associated health benefits which accompany fresh foods. Few grocery stores can compare with the taste and the value of fresh-picked vegetables or fruits. Canning and preserving permit us all to enjoy these foods while they are at their peak of freshness.

Lastly, we encounter the advantage provided to our dwindling pocketbook. There are certainly economic benefits related to canning and preserving your own foods that aren't found in relying upon store-bought provisions. We sleep in a time of troubled economic periods where every penny counts. Some families have managed to expand these pennies as they preserve and process their foods.

Deciding What's Right For You

Ready or not, here it comes! And no matter what "it" is, you will need food.

Food preservation--methods of keeping food in edible condition for any length of time--has been on the minds and in the hands of many of us for several years. Perhaps the first humans did not have to stress about it: fresh fruit, vegetables, nuts, and seeds probably were available year-round. But ever since the first apple went bad, people are trying various ways to save lots of food.

Given the present interest in and concern over natural disasters, man-made emergencies, food additives, and the end of the world, you may be brooding about survival food. Kits are available ready-made, but what if you want to do it yourself?

Maybe you have a kitchen garden or know an excellent farmers' market accessible. Or you have found a good deal on meat or had an exceptional hunting trip. Regardless, you want a way to preserve your bounty. So how does one do it? Canning? Freezing? Dehydrating? Another method?

These four tips can assist you in deciding which technique is true for you.

Survey your space

This includes areas for storing supplies, utensils, and equipment also because of the food that you preserve. Is there enough counter space for a dehydrator, pantry space for canners and jars, or cabinet space for freezer containers and wrap?

Search your schedule

How much time do you need to devote to your chosen technique? The quantity of your time needed for sorting, cleaning, preparing, and pre-treating foods, preparing equipment and supplies, and processing the food will vary according to the method. Do you have time for the whole canning or freezing process, or would the "load it and leave it" food dehydrating technique work better?

— **Scrutinize your financial state**

Certain costs are involved in each method, both initially and on-going. For instance, initial investments could also be a freezer, canner, or food dehydrator. On-going expenses include electricity or gas, jars, lids, storage or freezer bags, freezer containers, and paper or plastic wrap.

Study your situation

What shall you do with the food you preserve? Although this will sound sort of a strange question to ask, the solution has a crucial bearing pertaining to the food preservation methods you opt to use. Do you decide to keep it for years or use it as needed?

Will you cook it, eat it as it is, spread it on toast? Does it have to be portable? If you are hiking, wouldn't it be better to hold jars of canned foods, a cooler filled with frozen foods, or a backpack full of dehydrated food?

Consider space, schedule, state, and situation as your start line. There is a place for every of those food preservation methods; you will probably use more than one. Whatever you opt to do, make sure it is the right technique for you.

Sterilizing jars for canning

Sterilizing jars for canning is a crucial step in the home canning process. Although washing jars in hot soapy water are vital, it is not enough to make sure of a clean, germ-free environment. A second step is required to kill bacteria that may still be hanging around and make your jars are sterile and prepared to use for canning.

There are three easy ways to sterilize jars for canning. All three are effective and easy to do, so it is just a matter of preference (or space) on which one you use.

Boiling to Sterilize

The first method is to boil jars. To do this, you need a stockpot crammed with water. Place your jars in the stockpot and bring water to a boil. Boil for a minimum of 5 minutes. Remove with jar grabbers and place them upside-down on clean paper towels until ready to use. Or, if you would like to keep your jars hot until you use them, keep them in hot water (with the burner turned off) until ready to use and pull them out one at a time to fill.

Dishwasher Sterilizing

On the off chance that you have a dishwasher, this is regularly the best strategy. Just burden the containers into your dishwasher and run them through a cycle. Since numerous dishwashers require a long time to go through a washing/drying cycle, you need to plan to utilize this strategy. I normally start the dishwasher before I start my food prep and look at to time the dishwasher cycle ends once I need the containers.

A reward to the current strategy is that you are not utilizing important burner space while you are canning. It is likewise simple to keep your containers hot by leaving them in the dishwasher and hauling them out each in turn to utilize.

Oven Sterilizing

Since not every person has a dishwasher, nor do they have space to bubble pots while they are highly involved with canning, this third choice could be the awesome—'heat' your containers to clean them.

To utilize this technique, wash your containers with hot sudsy water and flush with heated water. Dry the containers and spot them upstanding on a stove rack. Turn the stove on to 225 degrees and permit containers to 'prepare' for 20 minutes. After the 20 minutes are up, I turn the broiler directly down to the base set, so the containers stay warm however aren't excessively hot to the touch to pull them out.

Purposes behind home canning and saving

There is an assortment of viable explanations behind home canning and saving. However, I'd wish to impart to you my own five main reasons why it is a smart thought to scan or save food at home. These are in no specific request except for are picked in light of the fact that I feel they make a great arrangement of clarifying why I appreciate home canning.

They additionally will reveal to you somewhat more about the motivation I adventure to keep me filling my storeroom with home-canned food.

Reason #1 - I Can Get Creative

It might appear to be somewhat on the cheesy side to some of you who purchase and burn-through canned jelly, yet I'm considering the number of you truly pause and take a long look at what is in the container you are getting a charge out of. I have painstakingly picked plans that end isn't just a delectable food thing yet additionally produce something outwardly engaging.

I love the manner in which a jam or jam can set with fixings caught in suspension. I additionally appreciate the different shading tints I can make just by modifying the sort of pepper I abuse in a formula.

These are a few stunts that permit me to be imaginative in how the completed item will look. Some of them set aside an effort to execute appropriately.

Reason #2 - Taste the norm

At the point when it includes home canning and protecting, there is no preferred taste over something that is natively constructed. Indeed, what I incline toward most about canning my own special jams, jams, hot sauces, and salsas is that I know precisely what fixings enter each container.

This means there are no additives or substance aggravates that have names that end with "... ose" in my items. Thus, this recommends the container of jam will be better for me. I really imagine that turns out in the flavor of each item I produce in the kitchen in my home.

Reason #3 - A Way Of Accomplishment

One part of home canning and protecting I really appreciate is the inclination I get following a day of working in the kitchen. The individual fulfillment I get from putting down a bunch of my top picks or from attempting another formula is energizing and fun. I locate that despite the fact that I just wind up canning a little clump of jams, I actually feel such an achievement. It seems as though I had finished an undertaking that isn't just testing however compensating too. As far as I might be concerned, one of my best five reasons would be this one because of how it assembles my certainty and adds to my stock simultaneously.

Reason #4 - Cost and Availability

As a viable explanation, the expense is a solid contention for home canning and safeguarding. It truly doesn't cost significantly at all to set yourself okay with canning at home. You need a few fundamental secrets to success, including an enormous canner for bubbling water, a rack to put inside the canner to line filled containers for preparing, containers, tops, and seals. As I rest in a piece of the country where naturally developed products of the soil are accessible in season, I purchase what I need for whatever formula I'm dealing with.

Close to the furthest limit of the period, I will have the option to buy my last fixings (generally at a discounted cost) and sweep them so I can appreciate the gathered harvests later in the year when there is no new product free. It implies I can simply go to my washroom any time in the year for something new that isn't loaded up with synthetic substances or has been mass-created.

Reason #5 - Inventory and Gifts

Since I have transformed home canning and protecting into somewhat locally situated business, at whatever point I can a group of something, most of the completed containers enter my stock; on the off chance that I wasn't loading up for business, I realize I may be utilizing a portion of my #1 plans as endowments. I do that with a portion of my unique items and have utilized them as home warming presents, something to take to supper at a companion's likewise concerning birthday events and uncommon events. I feel giving a current that is natively constructed has an uncommon significance, and if that blessing is a container of jam, it is even more an individual endowment of sharing.

Precautions When Canning Starchy Foods

Being busy with food safeguarding for quite a while, I have found that specific little-known techniques can help essentially in delivering a top-quality item. At the point when I initially started, I stumbled into numerous gossipy tidbits, which I eventually discovered to be bogus.

An illustration of this is the ability to can potatoes in my nourishments. All that I had perused recently seemed to show that I shouldn't add potatoes, noodles, or flour to any plans that I planned to can. I eventually found that there is no issue in canning potatoes either without help from anyone else or as a fixing.

The serious issue identified with potatoes spins around the sort of potatoes being canned. You may plan to can Russet or the preparing sort of potatoes, and they will at first look fantastic; nonetheless, in several brief months, they will rapidly go to mush and deteriorate, at long last settling unappetizingly to the lower part of the container.

Then again, the Yukon Gold assortment stays firm and engaging. What this uncovers to me is that while canning potatoes, one should utilize the "waxier" sorts rather than those considered being of a starch piece like found in the heating classification of potatoes.

Consequently, potatoes can really be canned either without anyone else or as an expansion to soups or stews without an issue. The point here is that in the event that you can utilize potatoes independently, there ought to be no explanation. They probably won't be canned close by different nourishments, moreover.

All things considered, I still never add potatoes to my soup that I make and can. What I do utilize is the thing that I allude to as a "Soup Starter Base." I will have the option to check the flavors, meat, onions; at that point, add the new vegetables like potatoes when I warm them, okay with serving at the table. Another favorable position of this technique is that it forestalls those different vegetables in the fixings list from tasting all very similar, especially following quite a while of sitting on a capacity rack.

Noodles of any sort present an extraordinary picture here and still shouldn't be canned. The USDA expresses that one shouldn't can pasta, any sort of thickeners (aside from Clear Gel, grain, or rice) because of the related consistency issues, which could end in lopsided warmth infiltration. You will fall upon certain individuals that guarantee to have securely utilized pasta or grain without any issues or issues. The decision will be up to you on the off chance that you are eager to take the possibility and you wouldn't fret soft noodles.

To clarify the consistency issue somewhat further, you should comprehend that warmth will experience meats because of the fat and water substance of the related food thing. The fat makes it a lot simpler for the warmth to enter the product. Crushed nourishments like pumpkin, winter squash, or potatoes don't have these required fats to assist with the warmth enter. These food sources normally have a thick-gluey consistency because of their starch content and tend to hinder the warmth entrance. While canning these food sources, utilize just lumps and not squashed.

Whenever canned as pieces, the potatoes should work out impressively. There are a few pieces of suggestion that should demonstrate significance in this regard. To start with, consistently utilize plain water and don't utilize the potato cooking water to top off your containers. To do so would yield an unappealing and super-bland item. The second clue I may wish to present to you is don't utilize chestnut potatoes. While white potatoes are absolutely fitted to canning, russets aren't.

Concerning utilizing the grain in soups, in the event that you need to, you should utilize close to 1 tablespoon of dry grain to at any rate one quart and no more. The grain is most likely going to gloat a significant sum, yet you keep on having adequate fluid in the soup container to supply a safe, smooth motion. The equivalent applies to pasta. In the event that you will utilize pasta in your soup, utilize the littlest sorts of pasta shapes as well as utilize only one tablespoon to a quart container.

It will be ideal if you remember that this entire cycle is conflicting to the USDA deciding that you shouldn't can with flour or flour related items. Ordinarily, as a substitute for canning flour, one can utilize "Clear Jel," which is an altered kind of cornstarch utilized as a thickener.

Try not to misconstrue me, for I completely uphold the USDA norms. However, we need to recall that they wish to decide in favor of security more than anything. Like anything throughout everyday life, one can't make one guideline that will apply to all or any circumstances. It is simpler to state definitely no flour or no pasta rather than to rely upon everybody realizing precisely what amount is sufficient in a formula. Hence, the USDA leaves us with mindful and expansive impediments.

Utilizing Citric Acid

These days, most are attempting to get in shape. A typical grumbling is that it is too costly to even consider keeping foods grown from the ground at your home. The time is short to the point that the product frequently turns sour before you get a chance to eat it. At that point, you need to discard it and purchase new stuff. However, it is debilitating, and may regularly want to squander cash. The vast majority simply head to the food path and pick unfortunate bites that advance weight gain and heart issues as opposed to learning approaches to safeguard solid, new food sources.

So how are you able to preserve those 'farmers market' foods so that you can keep them available for a healthy lifestyle? One popular method is 'canning.' Canning food is a good way to keep your products for a long time, neatly organized in your food cabinet. There are two ways to can: The boiling water method and the pressure canning method. Both are safe, and the method used will depend upon what food you are canning.

Low acid foods are often preserved by pressure cooking due to their pH levels (under 4.6). Higher acid foods (about 4.6), got to be preserved using the boiling water method. Here's where it gets tricky. If you have a food that is close to a 4.6 pH level, you will need to add acid to it. The reason high acid foods are often preserved just by using the boiling water method is that they need enough acid so that botulinus spores cannot grow their harmful, often deadly, toxin. Foods like tomatoes and figs need extra acid so that the time period can sustain in an environment without harmful growth on the food.

I've found citric acid to be the best additive to stop bacteria growth, both in canning and easy preservation of fruits, vegetables, and other foods. Whether or not you prefer to can is irrelevant. That is only one of the ways to keep your food fresher, for long. If you are just looking to add days to the time of your fruits or vegetables, you can add the acid directly, not needing any special type of processing or cans to keep the food fresh.

Many stores and websites sell acid to the typical consumer. Oftentimes it is packaged under the name 'sour salt.' It can come packaged looking like a spice in a shake container or by the bag. Some companies sell it by the pound, so you can get the most important bang for your buck. Buying by the pound will save money and allow you to use it for various things. Do your research, and you will find acid has multiple benefits far beyond food preservation.

Emergency Food

Simple, Safe, And Delicious

Preparing for emergencies is about survival, and one critical component to a survival strategy is emergency food. When planning for an emergency, you may prefer to include emergency food for a few weeks or a few decades, as freeze-dried disaster options include items with long shelf lives to supply necessary calorie and nutrient requirements over time.

A tremendous variety is packaged for easy storage and preparation. Whether you are looking to organize for yourself, a family, or maybe a large community, emergency food quantities are available to accommodate every appetite.

The variety is reflective of the vast array of food items in a grocery store. Perishable food items are preserved through canning, freeze-drying, dehydration, and vacuum seal technologies. Meats, fruits, vegetables, grains, and more are often purchased as part of a food storage supply. Numerous prepared meals are available in convenient packaging for breakfast, lunch, and dinner. For anyone trying to find an easy way to build a supply, ready-made kits are available for various time frames also as bulk storage.

Emergency food is meant for easy preparation, safe storage, and convenient portability. Meal pouches are handy for camping and hiking. They create smart additions to safety kits and rucksacks, providing necessary sustenance in the event that you become stranded while out and about. Following storm activity, grocery shelves are often bare, and power outages end in food spoilage when refrigeration fails. A supply of emergency food is a safe source of nourishment in these times.

For long-term survival strategies, food storage requires forethought and preparation. While many ready-to-eat options exist, many meals require the addition of water, and a few are self-heating also. The comfort of a hot meal in a difficult situation will provide sustenance for the body and spirit. A source of potable water is additionally a critical need for long-term survival, and a storage barrel or cans of emergency water are a practical addition. Items commonly are available individually packaged portions in weatherproof buckets.

Depending on the contents and preservation method, the time period of various items may vary. Most are safe for a minimum of five years, while many are safe for 10 years or more.

Longer shelf lives are practical for disaster preparation because you may plan for an emergency today that will not happen for years to come. The longer the time period of the food you store, the longer your emergency plans remain effective. Nutrition and energy are required for survival over time, and emergency food provides a viable source.

Natural Food Preservatives

Preserving food for a while was a necessity of mankind since time memorial. The supply of certain food items was limited to a specific season. Man's desire to use them throughout the year motivated him to create certain methods by which food items might be stored for a long duration without a big change in taste.

Food items are often categorized into perishable and non-perishable food items. Perishable items are those which get spoilt soon and are more susceptible to the attack of micro-organisms. Examples of some such items are vegetables, fruits, meat, eggs, milk, etc. these things have a really short time period. On the other hand, non-perishable foods are those which take a long duration to get spoilt, like rice, wheat, oils, dried pulses, etc.

The aim of using preservatives is to convert these perishable food items to non-perishable ones or extend the shelf-life. Food gets spoilt due to the attack of micro-organisms like bacteria, fungi, yeast, etc. they carry some undesirable chemical changes in the food. Food preservatives inhibit these chemical changes in various ways.

Food preservatives are of two types: natural and artificial, and both attempt to maintain the standard, edibility, and nutritive value of the foods.

Classification Of Natural Food Preservatives

Depending on their mode of action, food preservatives are broadly classified into three kinds.

- Antimicrobial preservatives that inhibit the expansion of the microorganisms

- Antioxidant preservatives inhibit the oxidation of food ingredients like fats, lipids, etc.

- Preservatives target the enzymes in the foodstuff and hence prevent natural activities like the ripening of food or post-harvest aging of foodstuff.

Some of the natural food preservatives include substances like salt, sugar, rosemary extract, essential oils, vinegar, etc. Out of those, substances like salt, sugar, and oils are used in our day-to-day life. Ongoing research is targeted towards the search for some new natural food preservatives. Let us discuss a few preservatives in detail.

Salt: Salt has been used to preserve food items like meat and fish for ages. At very high concentrations of salt, the cells of the micro-organisms lose water and dehydrate by the method of osmosis. It inhibits the expansion of bacteria, yeasts, and molds by the method of osmosis. Salting of meat preserves it for years. During pickling, raw mangoes, tomatoes, etc., are treated with considerably large amounts of salt. Even some vegetables like cabbage, cauliflower, and cucumber are often preserved by pickling them with salting.

Sugar: Sugar is a carbohydrate, and the mechanism by which it stores food is the same as that of salt. This substance also dehydrates the microorganisms by the method of osmosis. There are two ways in which the foodstuff is often stored in sugar.

1. Thick, concentrated syrup is often prepared, and the food substances are often immersed in it.

2. The food items are often cooked in sugar until sugar reaches the point of crystallization. A better concentration of sugar sweetens the food and either inhibits the expansion of microorganisms or kills them by the method of osmosis. Sugar is usually used to preserve fruits like apple, peach, pear, plum, etc., in the form of jams and jellies.

Vinegar: This acidic solution is ready by the fermentation of sugar and water solution. The method of fermentation is carried beyond the alcohol stage. Vinegar contains ethanoic acid, which kills the bacteria due to its acidity, or lower P.H. Vinegar is used to preserve meats and vegetables during pickling. Even in the method of canning, vinegar is used to extend the time of the food items.

Rosemary Extract: this is often prepared by the distillation of rosemary leaves and is known for its pleasant aroma and flavor. This substance has been used as a preservative for ages due to its antioxidant properties.

It prevents the oxidation of foodstuff, thus retaining the flavor and color of the food. The natural compounds present in the Rosemary extract like phenolic diterpenes, rosmarinic acid, and carnosol are liable for their antioxidant properties.

Some Traditional Practices Of Food Preservation

With the advancement in technology, man has conquered many difficult situations. In the olden days, means of transport weren't that efficient, and moreover, crops and vegetables grown in a particular area were considerably hooked into the seasonal conditions in that area. These conditions encouraged people at that point to adapt to certain practices, which helped them to preserve food throughout the year. E.g., Mango - Good raw mangoes are available only in the summer season. They will be preserved in several types of pickles. Aside from that, tiny mango pieces are often sundried after the application of salt. These mango pieces are often added to dhal throughout the year.

It is true that these days we get all the foodstuffs throughout the year with a variation in price. Fruits are no longer seasonal, and they are ripened with the assistance of chemicals like ethylene.

If we adopt these traditional practices in our day-to-day life, we will be able to face any kind of odd situation. Not only that, but we will prevent the wastage of giant quantities of food items also.

10 Uses For Used Canning Lids

Since it is hazardous to reuse a second-hand canning cover to seal another canning container, how to manage the entirety of the pre-owned tops? It is going not to seem, by all accounts, to be a tremendous issue for an intermittent home canner who sets up a couple of bunches of tomatoes, jam, and a jam every year.

In the event that you start canning a ton of stuff, you may wind up with a heap of utilized covers. Instead of tossing them into the garbage and adding to our landfill issues, here are ten imaginative thoughts for repurposing utilized canning tops.

1. Versatile

Shower paint the brilliant covers tones. Drill an opening through every cover a couple 1/4 of an in. from the edge. Bind the string to the top, then to the garments holder.

2. Coordinating game

Make an indistinguishable game. Print out two of each letter, numbers, pictures of creatures, shapes, colors, characters, and so on. Cut out the things and paste them to, in any event, one side of the cover.

3. Windchime

Drill a little opening close to the sting that is wide enough for the string to endure. Document off any unpleasant edges the boring piece made while drilling through the top. String them together at various levels yet close enough so they will contact each other. Alternatively, you can paint the covers in various tones prior to gathering.

4. Kids' toy

Drill a little opening close to the sting that is wide enough for the string to endure. Document off any unpleasant edges the boring piece made while drilling through the cover. Use string strip or string to integrate the covers. Try not to utilize any rusted covers or paint them. The paint could strip off.

5. Scarecrow

Clean the tops with #0000 wire fleece to give them a lovely brilliant sparkle. Drape them with a string around the nursery to ward the fowls off.

6. Fridge magnets

Print out family pictures. Slice them to suit the top. Paste the picture to the cover and a little level magnet on the rear of the top. They make incredible Christmas, birthday, and grandparent's day presents.

7. Blends in a container

Set up the dry blend for a most loved family formula (treat, cake, prepared beans, and so forth). Markdown retailers sell cheap canning containers. Fill the containers with the dry blend seal in with the utilized canning top and ring.

8. Dry Goods Storage

The pre-owned tops function admirably for fixing bricklayer containers packed with dry pasta, sugar, flour, noodles, and so forth. You needn't bother with a vacuum seal, just a sufficient seal to keep the residue and weevils out.

9. Christmas Yard Art

Drill or poke two little holes on the closures. Paint or buff the tops. String them together into strands. Another thought is to make a laurel with dropdowns of 3-5-7 from the most strand.

10. Christmas trimmings

Make a progression of Christmas decorations out of the tops by punching various examples into the top. Be inventive by punching in examples like snowmen, snowflakes, Santa Claus, Christmas tree, cross, and so forth. Take the ribbon and paste it to the surface circuit of the top.

Why Canning is Making a Comeback

Preserving processed food in airtight containers was invented in the late eighteenth century by the French military. It had been quite popular for several centuries until modern societies decided it had been easier to shop for their vegetables and food preserves ready-made at the supermarket.

Canning is a very efficient way to store foods for several years without the need for refrigeration. By properly sterilizing and preserving tomatoes, beans, strawberries, soup, etc., in glass jars, microorganisms cannot enter and proliferate inside the food. It is ideal to securely keep a large food supply, especially in areas where grocery stores are scarce.

Although canning lost a lot of its charm in the past few decades, it is now making a sensational comeback. The explanations for the increased popularity are obvious and is listed as follows:

1. Preserving your own crop - Starting a kitchen garden and planting fruit trees is a fun activity that will be enjoyed by everyone. Of course, once the crop is in, the food has to be stored, and the best way to achieve successful and lasting results is by canning.

2. Maintaining their standard of living - With wage freezes, job losses, and grocery prices skyrocketing, many of us try to save lots of on our grocery bills. By buying their canning supplies and products once they are on sale, they will actually produce meals cheaper than store-bought products.

3. Nutritional value - Nutritional awareness is consistently growing, exposing the harmful substances manufacturers use in their fruit, vegetable, and meat products. Acids, hormones, chemicals, and contaminants are often avoided by canning your own foods.

4. Health reasons - People with food allergies can make their own meals and keep a stash handy for the times they need no time to cook. Knowing what they are eating will prevent allergies.

5. Crackdown on foreign products - People do not want to consume imported foods, especially once they know that their country's own farmers can barely survive. Buying fresh produce that is in season at the green market and canning it for the offseason will support the local farmers.

6. Personal satisfaction - Canning your fruits, vegetables, and meats are often incredibly rewarding. Yes, there is a lot of labor involved, but at the end of the day, you will feel extremely satisfied with your accomplishments. Give it a try, and you will see!

Surviving the Upcoming Food Crisis

A growing population and rapid weather changes are causing issues with the food supply everywhere in the country. While there are reports about food shortages and a simultaneous rise in the cost of many products, many of us are unable to acknowledge this looming crisis. Much of this comes from the continued quick access to food that we enjoy, but that doesn't negate the dwindling of our resources.

Each summer shows more and more food shortages as droughts or floods hit farms while the demand for food continues to grow in developing worlds. While we have been producing an abundance of food for many years, enough to feed the whole world if managed properly, many food experts see us approaching the height of our food production.

Solutions to the present global food crisis will begin in every community's backyard. Small scale food production in the home will help to ease the food shortage and native hunger that threatens to overwhelm many.

There are some ways to make sure that you are going to be shielded from the approaching food crisis, and here are the top four.

Start a little Farm

Being able to supply your own food will become necessary for survival in the future, even as it used to be. If you do not know how to grow or raise your own food, it is easy to start out with small gardens of herbs and tomatoes in the beginning. Slowly expand what you have and what you are able to do until you have grown sufficiently.

This is not a task that is difficult no matter where you reside. While open pastures and enormous plots of land are the most fruitful, urban farms have started in the last decade.

You can create a whole functioning farm in a small plot of land with chickens and bees alongside your vegetables and fruits. If you do not know where to start out, sign up with your local co-op or gardening association to get assistance. They will also suggest good community gardens if you do not feel like you have the space necessary.

Learn to Preserve Your Food

Preserving your food is a time-honored tradition that takes

little or no time as long as you propose well. You can specialize in canning, pickling, or dehydrating foods to see how it feels for you.

While many tools will assist you during this process, you can either try it out with someone experienced in preservation or try it in your home.

For example, drying out food sources is less difficult in a dehydrator, yet you can likewise set your stove to 200 degrees F and have flavorful dried out apples in eight hours. You should eat tomatoes (this is the recommended novice's canning project because of the corrosiveness) in an enormous pot to try not to purchase a huge water shower.

Plan to get capable in-home safeguarding. Purchasing a decent dehydrator, pressure canner, vacuum sealer, or sun based controlled chest cooler will furnish you with the materials you need for long haul stockpiling.

Create a Mini-Store

Oldie but a goodie with Christopher Walken and Brendan Fraser makes them thing going for: the completely loaded store they arranged. This kind of capacity will work well for you while soaring food costs take steps to overpower you. An individual food bank is altogether more significant than a financial balance or bond. Choose foods with long shelf lives, like extra canned food and dried food. Pick up some food-grade bins to store bulk essentials like wheat, beans, and rice.

Pick up other essentials like sugar, salt, coffee, cooking oils, and spread, which are bound to go fast when supplies become limited. Consider what is essential for your nutrition and buy those items, because the worth will become astronomical, then add supplements and vitamins to your shelf.

Store Extra Seeds

There are different organizations, including various governments worldwide, that have stores of heirloom seeds in safe storage for the future. This is often for future plantings in the case of a world emergency or to preserve seeds that will become extinct shortly. This is often something that you should be doing also.

Seeds are often used as currency in the barter system and are necessary for your farm's long-term growth. Find out how to save lots of seeds from your healthiest plants to use for years in the future, ensuring genetic diversity in the vegetation and survival for your family.

Conclusion

Thank you once again for downloading *"Canning And Preserving: Preserving Foods At The Comfort Of Your Home."*

As referenced before in this guide, canning and safeguarding your own food is a financially savvy, productive approach to store vegetables and organic products you fill in your nursery. It is likewise an approach to safeguard some other bought nourishments for critical crossroads. With food costs rising, putting some new produce far off for bourgeoisie customers, developing and canning your own food is an approach to ensure that you can have sound, nutritious food if costs ascend to beyond what you can pay if food isn't accessible.

The savviest, life-expanding food conservation strategy is canning. Canning your food permits you to hold supplements that are lost through other safeguarding strategies like drying and freezing. Canned nourishments can keep going for quite a long while and aren't snared on to climate or forced accessibility. Food in your cooler is regularly valuable yet will turn sour in case of a force misfortune. Dried food sources just stay for such a long time before they begin to take on dampness again and are more powerless against bugs' pervasion.

What is the danger that you take once you can get your food at home? Your health and safety. You would like to recollect that this is often not something to gamble with - so being careful all the time is extremely important.

After you have canned and preserved your bountiful harvest, store it in a cool, dry place. Some foods will keep longer than others. One thing is certain, by growing and canning your own food, you and your family will always have a supply of nutritious, healthy foods in the event of a food shortage or natural disaster.

Now you know the things to do and to recollect on how to make preserves, it is now easy for you to do it at home. All are explained clearly, with no hassles. Homemade preserves are low in calories and fewer in preservatives. Making homemade preserves is additionally a good source of income and perhaps a perfect gift for your close friends. Try it now and enjoy the pleasures it brings on how to make preserves.

To your success!

Heather Lombard

Lightning Source UK Ltd.
Milton Keynes UK
UKHW021016160221
378868UK00001B/23